GOOGLE CHAT

FOR BEGINNERS

The Comprehensive Guide To Understanding And Mastering Google Chat For Communication, Exchange, And Collaboration Between Businesses And People

GOOGLE CHAT FOR BEGINNERS

The Comprehensive Guide To Understanding And Mastering Google Chat For Communication, Exchange, And Collaboration Between Businesses And People

GOOGLE CHAT FOR BEGINNERS: THE COMPREHENSIVE GUIDE TO UNDERSTANDING AND MASTERING GOOGLE CHAT FOR COMMUNICATION, EXCHANGE, AND COLLABORATION BETWEEN BUSINESSES AND PEOPLE

First edition. November 27, 2023.

Written by Voltaire Lumiere.

TABLE OF CONTENTS

CHAPTER 1
INTRODUCTION TO GOOGLE CHAT

- **What Is Google Chat?**

Google Chat, a versatile and robust communication platform, serves as a cornerstone in Google Workspace's suite of productivity tools. This application is designed to offer users a comprehensive and efficient means of real-time communication and collaboration. It's an evolution of Google Hangouts, providing a more streamlined and organized approach to messaging and interaction.

At its core, Google Chat is a text-based messaging tool that empowers users to exchange messages and have meaningful conversations with individuals or groups. It's a convenient way to keep in touch with colleagues, friends, or family, and it's deeply integrated into the Google ecosystem, making it an attractive choice for personal and professional communication needs.

Here are some of the key features and functionalities that define Google Chat:

1. Messaging and Group Conversations: Google Chat allows users to send and receive text messages in real time. You can initiate one-on-one conversations or create group chats for team discussions, project coordination, or social interactions. The chat interface is designed to be intuitive, enabling smooth and efficient communication.

2. Voice and Video Calls: In addition to text messaging, Google Chat offers voice and video calling capabilities. This means you can transition seamlessly from text-based discussions to audio or video calls, making it perfect for virtual meetings and quick consultations. Integration with Google Meet ensures high-quality video conferencing.

3. Shared Files and Documents: Sharing files, documents, and multimedia content is a breeze with Google Chat. Users can attach files, links, or documents directly within chat conversations. The integration with Google Drive allows for easy access to shared files and ensures that your documents are always up to date.

4. Customizable Profiles: Personalization is a significant aspect of Google Chat. You can customize your profile with a picture and a bio, making it easier for others to recognize and connect with you. It's an excellent way to establish your online identity within the chat environment.

5. Integration with Google Workspace: Google Chat seamlessly integrates with other Google Workspace apps like Google Calendar and Google Drive, enhancing your ability to collaborate and manage tasks. You can schedule meetings, view shared documents, and access your calendar directly from the chat interface.

6. Security and Privacy: Google Chat places a strong emphasis on security and privacy. It offers end-to-end encryption for one-on-one conversations to protect sensitive information. It also allows users to report and block suspicious activity, ensuring a secure communication environment.

7. Transition to Google Meet: One of the standout features of Google Chat is its integration with Google Meet. When your chat conversation evolves into a meeting, you can easily transition to a video call or virtual meeting, saving time and simplifying the process.

In summary, Google Chat is a versatile tool that simplifies communication, exchange, and collaboration, making it an indispensable component of the modern workspace. Whether you're connecting with colleagues, clients, or friends, Google Chat provides an integrated platform for seamless communication and collaboration, thereby enhancing productivity and streamlining workflow.

- **The Importance of Google Chat**

In the fast-paced digital landscape of today, effective communication is paramount, especially for businesses and individuals seeking to streamline their workflow and collaboration.

This is where Google Chat plays a vital role, offering several key aspects of importance that make it an essential tool in the modern era.

1. **Unified Communication Platform:** Google Chat is a unified platform for various modes of communication. It brings together text messaging, voice and video calls, and file sharing, allowing users to seamlessly switch between different communication methods within the same interface. This unified approach simplifies communication and reduces the need for multiple apps, saving time and enhancing efficiency.

2. **Enhanced Collaboration:** Collaboration is at the heart of any successful project or business. Google Chat's features, such as group chats and shared spaces, facilitate effective collaboration. Teams can exchange ideas, share files, and work on projects together, improving productivity and ensuring that everyone is on the same page.

3. **Integration with Google Workspace:** For businesses and professionals using Google Workspace, Google Chat is a critical tool for integrated productivity. It seamlessly integrates with other Google Workspace applications like Google Calendar, Google Drive, and Google Meet, providing a comprehensive ecosystem for work and communication. This integration streamlines processes, allowing users to access and manage their documents, schedules, and meetings with ease.

4. **Real-Time Communication:** In a world where immediacy is often a priority, Google Chat offers real-time communication. Whether it's a quick question to a colleague or an urgent team discussion, the ability to exchange messages and engage in voice or video calls in real time ensures that important matters can be addressed promptly.

5. **Remote Work and Virtual Meetings:** The global shift towards remote work and virtual meetings has been accelerated in recent years. Google Chat plays a significant role in facilitating these trends by providing a platform for remote teams to communicate effectively and host virtual meetings using Google Meet. This capability allows businesses to adapt to changing work environments and maintain productivity regardless of physical location.

6. **Personal and Professional Use:** Google Chat is versatile, serving both personal and professional communication needs. Individuals can use it to connect with friends and family, while businesses can leverage it for internal team communication and collaboration with clients and partners. This versatility makes Google Chat a one-stop solution for various communication scenarios.

7. **Security and Privacy:** Google Chat places a strong emphasis on security and privacy. It offers end-to-end encryption for one-on-one conversations, ensuring that sensitive information

remains secure. This focus on security is particularly important for businesses and organizations that handle confidential data.

8. **Simplicity and Ease of Use:** Google Chat is designed to be user-friendly and intuitive. Its clean interface and straightforward navigation make it accessible to users with varying levels of technical expertise. This simplicity reduces the learning curve and ensures that users can quickly adapt to the platform.

In summary, the importance of Google Chat lies in its ability to streamline communication, enhance collaboration, and adapt to the evolving landscape of remote work. Its integration with Google Workspace, combined with its real-time communication features and focus on security, makes it an invaluable tool for both personal and professional communication needs, ultimately improving productivity and fostering efficient teamwork.

- **Google Chat vs. Other Communication Tools**

In the realm of digital communication, there are various tools and platforms available, each with its unique features and advantages. Google Chat stands out as a versatile and powerful communication tool, and comparing it to other communication tools helps shed light on its distinctive attributes.

1. **Integration with Google Workspace:**

- Google Chat is seamlessly integrated with other Google Workspace apps such as Google Drive, Google Calendar, and Google Meet. This integration allows for a unified experience, making it easier to access and manage your documents, schedule meetings, and transition from chat to video calls. In contrast, some other communication tools may not offer such comprehensive integration.

2. **Real-Time Collaboration:**

- Google Chat excels in real-time collaboration. It offers features like group chats, shared spaces, and simultaneous document editing, making it an excellent choice for teams working together on projects. Some other tools may primarily focus on one aspect of communication, such as text messaging, and may not provide the same level of real-time collaboration.

3. **Unified Platform:**

- Google Chat's ability to handle text messaging, voice and video calls, and file sharing within a single platform makes it a unified solution for communication. Many other tools may require users to switch between multiple apps to achieve the same level of versatility, which can be less convenient and more time-consuming.

4. **Security and Privacy:**

- Google Chat offers robust security features, including end-to-end encryption for one-on-one conversations, helping to protect sensitive information. While other communication tools may have security measures in place, the level of security can vary. The commitment to privacy and data security is a notable advantage of Google Chat.

5. **Integration with Google Meet:**

- Google Chat seamlessly integrates with Google Meet, allowing users to transition from text-based conversations to video calls with ease. This integration simplifies the process of hosting virtual meetings, making it a strong choice for businesses and remote teams. Some other tools may require additional steps to switch from text to video communication.

6. **Simplicity and Familiarity:**

- Google Chat's user-friendly interface and the fact that it's part of the Google ecosystem make it a familiar and easily adaptable tool for those already using Google services. Users can leverage their existing Google accounts, reducing the need for additional setup. In contrast, other communication tools may require separate accounts and have steeper learning curves.

7. **Versatility for Personal and Professional Use:**

- Google Chat is versatile, serving both personal and professional communication needs. It is equally suitable for connecting with friends and family as it is for internal team communication and client interactions. This versatility sets it apart from tools that are primarily designed for specific use cases.

8. **Cost and Accessibility:**

- Google Chat is often available at no extra cost to users of Google Workspace, making it an economical choice for businesses already using Google's productivity suite. In comparison, some communication tools may come with subscription fees or usage restrictions, which can impact the cost-effectiveness of the solution.

In summary, Google Chat distinguishes itself through its integration with Google Workspace, real-time collaboration features, security and privacy measures, seamless integration with Google Meet, user-friendly interface, and versatility for both personal and professional use. While other communication tools have their strengths, Google Chat's comprehensive approach and seamless connectivity within the Google ecosystem make it a compelling choice for many users and businesses.

- **Setting Up Your Google Chat Account**

Setting up your Google Chat account is a straightforward process, and it's the first step towards harnessing the power of this versatile communication and collaboration tool. Here's a step-by-step guide to help you get started:

1. Accessing Google Chat:

- To set up your Google Chat account, you need a Google account. If you already have a Google account, you can proceed to the next steps. If not, you can create one by visiting the Google Account creation page and following the prompts.

2. Logging In:

- Once you have a Google account, go to the Google Chat website or access it through your Google Workspace or Gmail account. Log in with your Google account credentials.

3. Navigating to Google Chat:

- In your Gmail account, you can find Google Chat on the left sidebar. Click on the Chat icon to open the Chat interface. If you're using Google Workspace, your administrator may have already enabled Google Chat for your organization.

4. Customizing Your Profile:

- After logging in, take a moment to customize your profile. Click on your profile picture in the upper right corner and select "Settings." Here, you can add a profile picture, update your status, and set preferences according to your liking.

5. Adding Contacts:

- To start communicating, you'll need to add contacts. You can add contacts individually by entering their email addresses or import contacts from your Google Contacts. Click the "+" button in the Chat interface to add contacts or search for existing Google contacts.

6. Exploring the Chat Interface:

- Familiarize yourself with the Google Chat interface. You'll find your chat conversations on the left, contacts and groups in the middle, and your active chat on the right. The intuitive design makes it easy to navigate and start conversations.

7. Sending Your First Message:

- To initiate a chat, click on a contact or group, and a chat window will open. Type your message in the text box at the bottom and press "Enter" to send. You can also use emojis, share files, or start voice or video calls from the chat window.

8. Status and Presence:

- Google Chat allows you to set your status and presence. You can update your status to indicate if you're available, away, or busy. This helps your contacts know when it's a good time to reach out.

9. Notifications and Settings:

- Explore the notification and settings options to tailor Google Chat to your preferences. You can adjust notification settings, cnablc dcsktop notifications, and set up other preferences to make the tool work the way you want.

10. Mobile Access:

- If you want to access Google Chat on your mobile device, you can download the Google Chat app from your device's app store. Sign in with your Google account, and you'll have access to your chats on the go.

With these steps, you'll have your Google Chat account set up and ready to use. Google Chat provides an intuitive and user-friendly platform for communication and collaboration, whether you're connecting with colleagues, friends, or family.

- **Navigating the Google Chat Interface**

The Google Chat interface is designed to be user-friendly and intuitive, making it easy to navigate and manage your conversations. Here's a guide to help you become familiar with the various elements of the interface:

1. Chat List:

- When you first log in to Google Chat, you'll see your chat list on the left side of the screen. This list displays your ongoing conversations and contacts. You can see which of your contacts are online, and you can start new conversations by clicking on the "+" button at the bottom of the chat list.

2. Main Chat Window:

- The main chat window is located in the center of the interface. When you click on a contact or group from your chat list, the chat conversation opens here. You can send and receive messages, share files, and engage in voice or video calls within this window.

3. Contacts and Groups:

- In the middle section of the interface, you'll find your contacts and groups. Contacts are listed in alphabetical order, and you can easily search for specific contacts using the search bar at the top. Groups, such as teams or project groups, can be created and accessed here for efficient communication.

4. Profile Settings:

- Your profile picture is located in the upper-right corner of the interface. Click on your profile picture to access settings, where you can customize your profile, update your status, and configure your notification preferences.

5. Status and Presence:

- To let others know your current status or availability, click on your profile picture and select "Set Status." You can update your status to available, busy, away, or customize it with a specific message. Your status is visible to your contacts, helping them know when it's a good time to contact you.

6. Chat Features:

- Below the chat conversation in the main chat window, you'll find a set of icons and options. These features allow you to take various actions, such as sending files, starting voice or video calls, using emojis and reactions, and accessing settings for the specific chat.

7. Search Bar:

- At the top of the chat list, you'll find a search bar. This feature enables you to search for specific contacts, conversations, or keywords within your chat history. It's a handy tool for quickly locating past discussions or contacts.

8. Notifications:

- Notifications for new messages and updates appear in the bottom-right corner of the interface. You can click on these notifications to jump directly into the chat conversation. To adjust your notification settings, click on your profile picture and access the settings menu.

9. Additional Options:

- There are additional options available by clicking on your profile picture, such as accessing your settings, managing your Google Workspace account, and switching to other Google apps like Gmail or Google Meet. These options provide seamless navigation within the Google ecosystem.

The Google Chat interface is designed for simplicity and efficiency. It enables you to manage your chats, contacts, and conversations seamlessly, whether you're communicating with colleagues, friends, or family. The user-friendly design and intuitive layout make it easy to navigate and use the various features to enhance your communication and collaboration.

CHAPTER 2

GETTING STARTED WITH GOOGLE CHAT

- **Creating and Customizing Your Profile**

Your Google Chat profile is your digital identity in the world of online communication. Customizing your profile not only personalizes your presence but also makes it easier for your contacts to recognize and connect with you. Here's how you can create and customize your Google Chat profile:

1. Accessing Your Profile:

- Start by logging in to your Google Chat account. If you're using Google Chat within Gmail or Google Workspace, click on your profile picture in the upper right corner of the screen to access your profile settings. If you're using Google Chat as a standalone app, you can access your profile settings from the main interface.

2. Setting Your Profile Picture:

- A profile picture is often the first thing people notice about your profile. To set or change your profile picture, click on your current profile picture in the profile settings. You can upload a photo from your device, select one from Google Photos, or capture a new image using your device's camera.

3. Adding a Cover Photo (Optional):

- You can enhance your profile by adding a cover photo. While this step is optional, it can give your profile a more personalized and appealing touch. Click on the "Add Cover Photo" option and select an image from your device or Google Photos.

4. Editing Your Name:

- To customize your name, click on the "Name" field in your profile settings. You can modify your first and last name as they appear in your Google Chat profile. Make sure your name is accurate and recognizable to your contacts.

5. Customizing Your Status:

- Your status is a brief message that conveys your current availability or mood. You can customize your status to reflect your current situation or to add a personal touch to your profile. Click on the "Set Status" option and enter your desired message.

6. Adding Contact Information (Optional):

- Google Chat allows you to add contact information to your profile. This information can include your job title, department, and other details. It's optional but can be helpful, especially in a professional context, as it provides additional context about your role or responsibilities.

7. Saving Your Changes:

- After customizing your profile to your satisfaction, click the "Save" or "Done" button to save your changes. Your profile updates will be visible to your contacts and within your Google Chat interface.

8. Reviewing Your Profile:

- Take a moment to review your profile to ensure that all the changes you made are accurately reflected. This helps maintain a professional and consistent online presence.

Your customized Google Chat profile allows you to present yourself authentically in your online interactions, whether you're connecting with colleagues, clients, friends, or family. The profile picture, cover photo, name, status, and optional contact information provide a well-rounded picture of your digital identity, making it easier for others to recognize and communicate with you effectively.

- **Adding Contacts and Groups**

Building a contact list and creating groups in Google Chat is essential for efficient and organized communication. Here's how to add contacts and create groups in Google Chat:

Adding Individual Contacts:

1. **Access Google Chat:** Log in to your Google Chat account, and access the main interface.

2. **Search for Contacts:** To add individual contacts, use the search bar at the top of the chat list. Type in the name or email address of the person you want to add.

3. **Send a Chat Request:** Click on the contact's name in the search results. A chat window will open. To add them to your contacts, you can send a chat request by typing a message or simply clicking the "Send Invite" button. The contact will receive the invitation to connect.

4. **Accepting Contact Requests:** If someone sends you a contact request, you will receive a notification. Click on the notification to review the request, and you can accept or decline it. Once accepted, the person will be added to your contacts.

Creating Groups:

1. **Access Google Chat:** Make sure you're logged in to your Google Chat account and have access to the main interface.

2. **Click on the "+" Button:** In the chat list on the left, click the "+" button at the bottom. This will open the "Create group" dialog.

3. **Add Members:** In the "Create group" dialog, start typing the names or email addresses of the contacts you want to add to the group. Google Chat will suggest matches from your existing contacts. Select the contacts you want to include in the group.

4. **Customize Group Details:** You can customize the group's name and add a group photo if desired. Additionally, you can set the group's access, which can be "Anyone in your organization" or "Anyone with the link" for broader accessibility.

5. **Create the Group:** After customizing the group's details, click the "Create" button. The group will be created, and all selected members will be added to it.

6. **Group Settings:** Click on the group in your chat list to access its settings. You can manage group settings, such as group notifications, changing the group's name, or adding or removing members, by clicking on the group name.

By adding individual contacts and creating groups in Google Chat, you can easily manage your communication with colleagues, friends, and family. Groups are especially useful for team collaboration or connecting with specific sets of contacts efficiently. Building and maintaining a well-organized contact list simplifies your interactions and ensures you can reach out to the right people at the right time.

- **Sending Your First Message**

Once you've set up your Google Chat account, added contacts, and customized your profile, it's time to send your first message. Sending a message in Google Chat is a simple process. Here's how to do it:

1. Access Google Chat:

- Start by logging in to your Google Chat account. You can access Google Chat via Gmail or the standalone app.

2. Open a Chat Conversation:

- In the chat list on the left side of the interface, click on the contact's name or the group you want to send a message to. This will open a chat conversation in the main chat window in the center of the screen.

3. Compose Your Message:

- In the chat conversation, you'll see a text box at the bottom of the window. Click inside the text box to start composing your message.

4. Type Your Message:

- Type your message in the text box. You can write a greeting, ask a question, or simply start the conversation with whatever message you'd like to send.

5. Send Your Message:

- To send your message, press the "Enter" key on your keyboard. The message will be sent to the contact or group, and it will appear in the chat conversation. If you prefer to use a button to send the message, you can usually find a "Send" or "Paper Plane" icon near the text box.

6. Emojis and Reactions (Optional):

- If you want to add a little extra expression to your message, you can use emojis and reactions. Google Chat allows you to select from a variety of emojis and reactions to respond to messages in chat conversations. Simply click on the emoji or reaction icon to choose from the available options.

7. Attach Files (Optional):

- You can also attach files or documents to your messages in Google Chat. Look for the paperclip or attachment icon, click on it, and then select the file you want to share. This can be a document, image, video, or any file you need to send.

8. Voice and Video Calls (Optional):

- If your chat conversation evolves into a need for voice or video communication, you can initiate a call by clicking on the voice or video call icons in the chat conversation. This allows you to seamlessly transition from text-based communication to real-time calls.

9. Continue the Conversation:

- Once you've sent your first message, you can continue the conversation by responding to the replies from your contact or group. Google Chat keeps the conversation thread organized and easily accessible.

By following these steps, you can send your first message in Google Chat and begin engaging in real-time text-based communication with your contacts. Whether you're using it for professional or personal purposes, Google Chat's user-friendly interface makes it easy to connect with others and collaborate efficiently.

- **Understanding Status and Presence**

Status and presence indicators in Google Chat play a crucial role in effective communication. They provide information about a user's availability, making it easier for others to know when it's an appropriate time to contact them. Here's an explanation of status and presence in Google Chat:

1. Status:

- Status in Google Chat reflects your current availability or mood. It is typically displayed alongside your profile picture or name, and it can be customized to convey various messages. Here are some common status options and their meanings:

- **Available:** This status indicates that you're online and ready to chat. It's the default status when you're actively using Google Chat.

- **Busy:** Use this status to signal that you're occupied or in the middle of a task and may not be able to respond immediately.

- **Away:** When you're not actively using Google Chat or your device is idle, your status may change to "Away" to inform others that you're not currently available.

- **Custom Status:** You can create a custom status to provide specific information about your availability or what you're currently working on. This allows you to personalize your status message.

- **Inactive:** If you've been idle for a certain period, Google Chat may automatically set your status to "Inactive" to inform others that you might not be responsive.

2. Presence:

- Presence indicators are visual cues that show whether your contacts are currently online and available to chat. They are displayed in the chat list, helping you quickly identify who is accessible. Here are the presence indicators:

- **Green Dot:** A green dot next to a contact's name signifies that they are currently online and available to chat.
- **Gray Dot:** A gray dot means the contact is not actively using Google Chat or is idle. They may not be immediately responsive.
- **Empty Circle:** An empty circle icon next to a contact's name indicates that they have set a custom status. You can hover over the icon to view their custom status message.

Understanding status and presence in Google Chat helps you determine the best times to initiate conversations with your contacts. It's a convenient way to respect their availability and engage in productive and considerate communication.

By setting an accurate status and being mindful of the presence indicators of your contacts, you can create a more efficient and respectful communication environment in Google Chat, whether you're using it for work-related discussions or personal interactions.

- **Using Emojis and Reactions**

Emojis and reactions are expressive tools that add a personal touch to your messages in Google Chat. They enable you to convey emotions, acknowledge messages, and engage with your contacts in a fun and engaging way. Here's how to use emojis and reactions in Google Chat:

Emojis:

1. **Access the Emojis:** When you're in a chat conversation, you'll find the emoji icon in the chat input area. It's usually represented by a smiley face or an emoji icon.

2. **Select an Emoji:** Click on the emoji icon to open the emoji picker. You'll see a wide array of emojis to choose from. Emojis are organized into various categories, making it easy to find the one that best suits your message.

3. **Search for Emojis (Optional):** If you have a specific emoji in mind, you can use the search bar within the emoji picker to quickly find it. Simply type a keyword or description, and relevant emojis will appear.

4. **Insert the Emoji:** Click on the emoji you want to use, and it will be added to your message in the chat conversation. The emoji will appear exactly where your cursor is placed in the text box.

5. **Send Your Message:** After inserting the emoji, you can add any additional text or content you'd like to include in your message. Once you're satisfied, press "Enter" or click the "Send" button to send your message with the emoji.

Reactions:

1. **React to a Message:** In Google Chat, you can react to specific messages with emojis. Hover your mouse pointer over a

message, and you'll see a smiley face icon (or an emoji icon) appear to the right.

2. **Click the Reactions Icon:** Click on the reactions icon, and an emoji picker will open. Here, you can choose the emoji that best represents your reaction to the message. Click on the emoji to select it.

3. **View Reactions:** After you've reacted to a message, your selected emoji will appear next to the original message, indicating your response. Other participants in the chat can also see the reactions added by different users.

4. **Modify or Remove Reactions:** If you want to change your reaction or remove it, simply click the reactions icon again and select a different emoji or click the "Remove" option.

Using emojis and reactions in Google Chat adds a layer of expressiveness and interactivity to your conversations. Whether you're celebrating an achievement, expressing empathy, or simply having fun in a chat, these features enable you to communicate with more nuance and emotion. Emojis and reactions can also foster a positive and engaging atmosphere in both personal and professional conversations.

CHAPTER 3

CHAT FEATURES AND FUNCTIONALITY

- **Text Chat and Group Messaging**

Text chat and group messaging are core features of Google Chat that enable users to engage in real-time text-based conversations with individuals and teams. Here's an overview of how to use text chat and group messaging in Google Chat:

Text Chat:

1. **Starting a One-on-One Chat:**

- To initiate a one-on-one chat, locate the contact you want to message in your chat list on the left side of the interface. Click on their name to open a chat conversation in the main chat window. You can start typing your message in the text box at the bottom and hit "Enter" to send it.

2. **Sending Messages:**

- In the chat conversation, you can send text messages to your contact. Messages are delivered in real-time, and you can send multiple messages in a row to continue the conversation.

3. **Receiving Messages:**

- When your contact responds, their messages will appear in the chat window. You can read and respond to them as they come in.

4. **Attachments and Media Sharing:**

- You can share files, images, and other media in a one-on-one chat. To do this, click on the attachment or media icon in the chat conversation, select the file or image you want to share, and send it.

5. **Voice and Video Calls:**

- In a one-on-one chat, you can initiate voice or video calls by clicking on the respective icons in the chat conversation. This allows you to transition from text-based communication to real-time calls.

Group Messaging:

1. **Creating a Group:**

- To start a group chat, click on the "+" button at the bottom of the chat list. Select "Create group," and then add the contacts you want to include in the group. Customize the group name and photo, and click "Create" to create the group.

2. **Sending Messages in a Group:**

- In a group chat, you can send messages that are visible to all participants. Type your message in the chat text box and hit "Enter." The message will be sent to the entire group.

3. **Attachments and Media Sharing in Groups:**

- Similar to one-on-one chats, you can share files, images, and media in group chats. Click on the attachment or media icon, select the file or image, and send it to the group.

4. **Reactions and Mentions:**

- In group chats, you can use reactions to respond to messages with emojis. You can also mention specific participants in the group by typing "@" followed by their name to get their attention.

5. **Managing Group Participants:**

- You can manage group participants by clicking on the group in your chat list. Here, you can add or remove members, change the group settings, or leave the group if you're the creator.

Text chat and group messaging in Google Chat provide a versatile and effective way to communicate with individuals and teams, whether for work-related discussions, project collaboration, or casual conversations with friends and family. These features facilitate real-time interactions, sharing of information, and collaboration, making it a valuable tool for various communication needs.

- **Voice and Video Calls**

Google Chat offers the ability to make voice and video calls, providing a seamless transition from text-based communication to real-time audio and video interactions. Here's how to make voice and video calls in Google Chat:

Voice Calls:

1. **Initiating a Voice Call:**

- In a one-on-one chat or group chat, you can initiate a voice call by clicking on the phone icon. This icon is usually located in the top right corner of the chat conversation.

2. **Connecting to the Call:**

- When you click the phone icon, Google Chat will establish the voice call. Your contact will receive an incoming call notification and can choose to answer or decline the call.

3. **Conducting the Call:**

- Once the call is connected, you can engage in a voice conversation with your contact. You can use this feature for conversations where audio communication is more convenient or necessary.

4. **Ending the Call:**

- To end the call, you can click the "End Call" button or icon within the call interface. Your contact will also have the option to end the call on their side.

Video Calls:

1. **Starting a Video Call:**

- In a one-on-one chat or group chat, you can initiate a video call by clicking on the video camera icon. This icon is usually located in the top right corner of the chat conversation.

2. **Connecting to the Video Call:**

- When you click the video camera icon, Google Chat will establish the video call. Your contact will receive an incoming call notification and can choose to answer or decline the call.

3. **Participating in the Video Call:**

- Once the video call is connected, you can engage in a video conversation with your contact. Both participants can see each other via their device's cameras and have the option to mute or unmute their microphones.

4. **Ending the Video Call:**

- To end the video call, you can click the "End Call" button or icon within the call interface. Your contact can also end the call on their side. Video calls in Google Chat offer the ability to communicate more intimately and conduct virtual face-to-face meetings.

Transitioning from Text Chat to Calls:

Google Chat seamlessly allows you to transition from a text-based conversation to voice or video calls. If you're in a chat conversation and wish to switch to a call, simply click the phone or video camera icon to initiate the desired call. This convenience streamlines communication and enables you to choose the most appropriate mode of interaction for your conversations.

Voice and video calls in Google Chat enhance the depth and personalization of your communication, whether it's for professional meetings, staying in touch with loved ones, or collaborating with colleagues. The ability to seamlessly transition from text chat to calls makes it a versatile tool for a wide range of communication needs.

- **Sharing Files and Documents**

Sharing files and documents in Google Chat is a convenient way to exchange information, collaborate on projects, and enhance communication. Here's how to share files and documents in Google Chat:

1. Accessing the Chat Conversation:

- To share a file or document, start by opening a chat conversation with the person or group you want to share it with. Click on the contact or group in your chat list to access the chat window.

2. Sharing a File:

- Within the chat conversation, locate the attachment or paperclip icon (this may vary slightly depending on your device or interface). Click on this icon to open the file attachment dialog.

3. Choose a File to Share:

- In the file attachment dialog, you can select a file or document to share. You can either upload a file from your device, select a file from your Google Drive, or choose from recent files.

4. Uploading from Your Device:

- If you're uploading a file from your device, click on the "Upload" or "Select from device" option. Browse your computer or mobile device to locate and select the file you want to share. Click "Open" or "Upload" to confirm your selection.

5. Selecting from Google Drive:

- If the file you want to share is stored in your Google Drive, click on the "Drive" or "Select from Drive" option. This will open your Google Drive, and you can choose the file you want to share. Click "Insert" or "Select" to add the file to the chat.

6. Sharing the File:

- Once you've selected the file to share, click the "Send" or "Share" button. The file will be sent in the chat conversation.

7. Accessing the Shared File:

- Your contact or group members will receive the shared file in the chat conversation. They can click on the file to view or download it, depending on the file type and permissions.

8. Viewing File Details:

- If you want to view more information about the shared file, you can click on the file in the chat conversation to open the file details. This includes file name, size, and access options.

9. Receiving Notifications:

- When a file is shared with you in a chat, you'll receive a notification in Google Chat, making it easy to access and interact with the shared file.

10. Collaboration and Editing (Google Workspace):

- If you're using Google Workspace, files shared from Google Drive can be collaboratively edited in real time. You can invite others to collaborate on the file by clicking the "Open in Google

Docs/Sheets/Slides" option, depending on the file type. This allows multiple users to edit the file simultaneously.

Sharing files and documents in Google Chat is a powerful feature for both personal and professional communication. It streamlines collaboration and enables quick information exchange, making it easier to work on projects, share important documents, or simply send photos and media to friends and family.

- **Integrating Google Chat with Other Google Apps**

One of the key strengths of Google Chat is its seamless integration with various other Google Apps and services. This integration enhances your productivity, streamlines communication, and allows you to access and share information across the Google ecosystem. Here's how to integrate Google Chat with other Google Apps:

1. Google Workspace Integration:

- If your organization uses Google Workspace (formerly G Suite), Google Chat is seamlessly integrated with other apps in the suite, such as Gmail, Google Drive, Google Calendar, and Google Meet. This integration enhances collaboration and productivity for businesses and teams.

2. Gmail Integration:

- Google Chat is tightly integrated with Gmail. In Gmail, you can access Google Chat on the left sidebar. It provides a unified interface for managing your email and chat conversations. You can easily switch between email and chat to communicate with your contacts without leaving the Gmail platform.

3. Google Drive Integration:

- Google Chat is connected to Google Drive, which means you can share and collaborate on Google Drive files and documents directly within a chat conversation. You can share Google Drive files by clicking the attachment icon in the chat conversation.

4. Google Calendar Integration:

- Google Chat integrates with Google Calendar, making it easy to schedule meetings and appointments with your contacts. You can access your Google Calendar events within the Google Chat interface and initiate video meetings using Google Meet.

5. Google Meet Integration:

- Google Chat is tightly integrated with Google Meet, Google's video conferencing platform. You can start a video call directly from a chat conversation by clicking the video call icon. This seamless integration allows you to transition from text-based chat to video meetings effortlessly.

6. Google Contacts Integration:

- Your Google Chat contacts are synchronized with your Google Contacts. This means that the contacts you add or communicate with in Google Chat are also accessible in other Google Apps, making it easy to reach out to them via email or other channels.

7. Google Workspace Add-Ons:

- Google Workspace provides add-ons that can further enhance the functionality of Google Chat. These add-ons, available from the Google Workspace Marketplace, allow you to integrate third-party apps and services for specific tasks and workflows.

8. Mobile Apps Integration:

- Google Chat has mobile apps available for both Android and iOS. These apps are integrated with your device's capabilities, allowing you to receive notifications and stay connected while on the go.

9. Google Assistant Integration:

- Google Chat can integrate with Google Assistant for voice commands and tasks. You can use voice commands to send messages, make calls, or perform other actions within Google Chat.

10. Third-Party Integrations:

- While Google Chat is designed to work seamlessly with Google Apps, you can also explore third-party integrations through the Google Chat API and other developer tools to connect with external services and apps.

Integrating Google Chat with other Google Apps creates a cohesive ecosystem for communication, collaboration, and productivity. It allows you to work more efficiently, share information effortlessly, and switch between tasks and applications with ease, whether you're managing your calendar, sharing documents, or conducting video meetings. This integration simplifies the way you communicate and work within the Google environment.

- **Setting Notifications and Customizing Chat Settings**

Customizing notifications and chat settings in Google Chat is crucial for tailoring the platform to your specific needs. It allows you to control how you receive alerts, organize your conversations, and manage your preferences. Here's how to set notifications and customize chat settings in Google Chat:

1. Accessing Chat Settings:

- Start by logging in to your Google Chat account and accessing the main chat interface. To customize settings, click on your profile picture in the upper-right corner and select "Settings."

2. General Settings:

- **Theme:** You can choose between light and dark themes to personalize the appearance of Google Chat.
- **Conversation View:** Select whether you want chat conversations to be grouped by people or displayed as separate threads.
- **Idle Notifications:** Enable or disable notifications when you're idle.

3. Notifications Settings:

- **Notifications:** Customize how you receive notifications. You can choose to receive notifications for new messages, mentions, and more. Options typically include:
  - New messages
  - @mentions
  - Group mentions
  - Reactions to your messages
  - Incoming calls
  - Scheduled events
  - Focus on notifications for important conversations
- **Notification Sound:** Choose a sound for incoming notifications.

- **Notification Banner:** Decide whether you want banners to appear when you receive notifications.
- **Desktop Notifications:** Enable or disable desktop notifications, which appear outside the chat interface.

4. Chat History Settings:

- **Chat History:** Determine how long you want to keep chat history. You can choose to keep it forever, for a specific number of days, or to delete it automatically.
- **Save Forwarded Messages:** Specify whether you want to save forwarded messages in your chat history.
- **Export Chat History:** You can export your chat history to a file for archiving purposes.

5. Keyboard Shortcuts:

- Explore keyboard shortcuts that can help you navigate and use Google Chat more efficiently.

6. Mobile Settings (if using mobile apps):

- If you're using the mobile app, you may find additional settings for notifications and chat customization. These settings are typically available in the app's preferences or settings menu.

7. Save Changes:

- After customizing your chat settings and notification preferences, be sure to save your changes by clicking the "Save" or "Done" button.

By customizing your notifications and chat settings, you can tailor Google Chat to your specific preferences and requirements. This ensures that you receive alerts and information in a way that aligns with your workflow and communication style. Whether you prefer to keep your chat history organized or want to control the types of notifications you receive, Google Chat provides the flexibility to match your needs.

CHAPTER 4
MANAGING CONVERSATIONS

- **Organizing Chats and Conversations**

Efficiently organizing your chats and conversations in Google Chat is essential for managing your communications, whether it's for personal, professional, or team-related discussions. Here are some tips on how to keep your chats and conversations organized in Google Chat:

1. Chat List:

- Your chat list, located on the left side of the interface, is where you'll find your ongoing conversations and contacts. To organize your chat list:

- **Pin Important Chats:** You can pin important chats to keep them at the top of your list. Click on a chat, then click the pin icon to the left of the contact's name to pin it. Pinned chats are easy to access and stand out.

- **Star Conversations:** You can star specific conversations by clicking on the star icon in the chat list. This is helpful for marking important or frequently accessed chats.

- **Group Chats:** Create or join group chats to keep related conversations and topics organized in one place. Group chats are perfect for team collaboration or specific projects.

2. Archiving Chats:

- Instead of deleting chats, you can archive them to declutter your chat list. Archived chats are still accessible but are moved to the "Archived" section. To archive a chat, right-click on the chat in the chat list and select "Archive."

3. Search Function:

- Google Chat has a robust search function. You can use the search bar at the top of the chat list to find specific conversations, contacts, or keywords. This is handy for quickly locating past discussions.

4. Labels and Filters (Google Workspace):

- If you're using Google Workspace, you can use labels and filters to automatically categorize and organize your chats. For example, you can set up filters to label chats from specific contacts or with specific keywords.

5. Mute Chats:

- If you're part of a chat that's less relevant or active, you can mute the chat to stop receiving notifications. Right-click on the chat in the chat list and select "Mute."

6. Custom Status:

- You can set custom statuses in your chats to indicate your availability or provide additional context to your contacts. This helps in organizing your interactions by signaling your current status or mood.

7. Manage Group Chats:

- If you're part of multiple group chats, make sure to manage them effectively. You can rename groups, add or remove members, and adjust group settings by clicking on the group name in the chat list.

8. Use Emojis and Reactions:

- In group chats, using emojis and reactions can help acknowledge messages, convey emotions, and keep the conversation engaging and organized.

9. Communication Etiquette:

- Encourage clear and concise communication within your chats. Use descriptive chat titles and message subjects to help keep conversations organized.

10. Declutter Regularly:

- Periodically review your chat list and archived chats to declutter and remove chats you no longer need. This keeps your chat interface tidy and efficient.

11. Integrated Apps:

- Take advantage of integrated apps and services within Google Chat for task management, file sharing, or note-taking to keep related content organized.

Efficiently organizing your chats and conversations in Google Chat helps you stay focused and productive in your communication. By applying these tips and utilizing the built-in features of Google Chat, you can maintain a tidy and functional chat environment for both personal and professional use.

- **Pinning Important Chats**

Pinning important chats in Google Chat is a useful feature that allows you to keep your most crucial and frequently accessed conversations at the top of your chat list for quick and easy access. Here's how to pin important chats in Google Chat:

1. Access Google Chat:

- Start by logging in to your Google Chat account and accessing the main chat interface.

2. Locate the Chat to Pin:

- In your chat list on the left side of the interface, find the chat that you want to pin. This could be a one-on-one chat with a contact or a group chat.

3. Pin the Chat:

- To pin a chat, simply click on the chat to open it. Then, look for the pin icon, usually located to the left of the contact or group name. Click on the pin icon.

4. View Pinned Chats:

- Once you've pinned the chat, it will move to the top of your chat list, above the unpinned chats. Pinned chats are easy to identify because they have a pin icon next to them.

5. Unpin a Chat (Optional):

- If you ever want to unpin a chat, follow the same process. Click on the chat you've pinned, and then click the pin icon again to remove the pin.

Pinning important chats is a simple but effective way to keep your most essential conversations easily accessible. Whether you need to stay connected with colleagues, clients, or friends, pinning chats helps you prioritize and organize your interactions within Google Chat.

- **Archiving and Searching Chats**

Archiving and searching chats in Google Chat are important functions that help you keep your chat list organized and easily retrieve past conversations. Here's how to archive and search chats in Google Chat:

Archiving Chats:

1. **Access Google Chat:**

- Start by logging in to your Google Chat account and accessing the main chat interface.

2. **Archiving a Chat:**

- To archive a chat, locate the chat you want to archive in your chat list on the left side of the interface.

3. **Archive the Chat:**

- Right-click on the chat or click on the three vertical dots (more options) icon next to the chat. In the dropdown menu, select "Archive." The chat will be moved to the "Archived" section of your chat list.

4. **View Archived Chats:**

- To access your archived chats, scroll down your chat list to the "Archived" section. Click on it to reveal your archived chats. You can click on any archived chat to view its contents.

5. **Unarchiving a Chat (Optional):**

- To unarchive a chat and move it back to your main chat list, simply click on the chat from the "Archived" section, and it will be restored to your chat list.

Searching Chats:

1. **Access Google Chat:**

- Log in to your Google Chat account and access the main chat interface.

2. **Use the Search Bar:**

- At the top of the chat interface, you'll find a search bar. Click in this bar to activate the search feature.

3. **Enter Keywords:**

- Type keywords, contact names, or phrases related to the chat you're looking for. Google Chat will start displaying relevant results as you type.

4. **Review Search Results:**

- As you type your search query, Google Chat will display search results in real-time. You can click on a result to view the full chat conversation.

5. **Use Filters (Optional):**

- To refine your search results, you can use filters. Click on the "Filters" button that appears to the right of the search bar. You can filter by chat type, contact, or date range to narrow down your results.

6. **Clear Search:**

- After you've completed your search, you can click the "X" icon in the search bar to clear your search and return to your main chat list.

Archiving and searching chats in Google Chat is an efficient way to maintain a clean and organized chat list while still being able to access past conversations when needed. This feature ensures that you can find and review important information or discussions quickly, whether you're looking for work-related details, personal messages, or anything in between.

- **Muting and Blocking Contacts**

Muting and blocking contacts in Google Chat are important functions that allow you to control your interactions and maintain a comfortable chat environment. Here's how to mute and block contacts in Google Chat:

Muting Contacts:

Muting a contact means that you won't receive notifications for their messages. This is helpful when you want to temporarily silence a conversation or if a contact is sending frequent messages that you don't want to be immediately alerted to.

1. **Access Google Chat:**

- Start by logging in to your Google Chat account and accessing the main chat interface.

2. **Select the Chat to Mute:**

- Locate the chat with the contact you want to mute in your chat list.

3. **Mute the Chat:**

- Right-click on the chat or click on the three vertical dots (more options) icon next to the chat. In the dropdown menu, select "Mute conversation." This will silence notifications for that specific chat.

4. **Unmuting a Chat (Optional):**

- To unmute the chat and start receiving notifications again, follow the same process. Right-click on the chat or use the more options menu, and select "Unmute conversation."

Blocking Contacts:

Blocking a contact means that they can't send you messages or interact with you in Google Chat. This can be useful for blocking unwanted or harassing messages.

1. **Access Google Chat:**

- Log in to your Google Chat account and access the main chat interface.

2. **Select the Chat to Block:**

- Locate the chat with the contact you want to block in your chat list.

3. **Block the Contact:**

- Right-click on the chat or click on the three vertical dots (more options) icon next to the chat. In the dropdown menu, select "Block." This will block the contact from sending you messages.

4. **Unblocking a Contact (Optional):**

- To unblock the contact, you'll need to access your Google Account settings. This is typically done through your Google Account settings, as blocking contacts isn't reversible directly from Google Chat.

Blocking contacts should be used judiciously, as it prevents all communication with the blocked contact. It's a helpful feature when dealing with harassment or unwanted messages, but it's important to be aware of its implications.

Muting and blocking contacts in Google Chat provide you with the flexibility to manage your chat interactions effectively. These features help you maintain a peaceful and controlled chat environment while still allowing you to engage with those who matter to you.

- **Exporting Chat History**

Exporting your chat history in Google Chat allows you to keep a record of your conversations or move your chat data to another platform or storage location. Here's how to export your chat history:

1. Access Google Chat:

- Log in to your Google Chat account and access the main chat interface.

2. Open the Chat Conversation:

- Locate the chat conversation that you want to export. Click on the chat to open it.

3. Access Chat Options:

- In the chat conversation, click on the three vertical dots (more options) icon, usually located in the top right corner of the chat window.

4. Export Chat:

- In the dropdown menu, select "Export chat." This will initiate the process of exporting the chat history.

5. Choose the Export Format:

- You'll be prompted to choose the format in which you want to export the chat. Google Chat typically offers options like "PDF" or "Text file" for exporting the chat content.

6. Save the Exported File:

- After selecting the export format, you can choose the destination where the exported file will be saved on your device. Browse your computer or mobile device to select the location, and provide a name for the file.

7. Save or Download:

- Click "Save" or "Download" to save the chat history in the chosen format to the specified location.

8. Repeat as Needed:

- If you have multiple chats you want to export, you can repeat this process for each one individually.

Please note that the ability to export chat history may depend on your organization's Google Chat settings and permissions. It's also essential to respect privacy and confidentiality when exporting chat content, especially in a business or professional context.

Exporting chat history is a valuable feature that allows you to create backups of important conversations, archive discussions for future reference, or migrate your chat data to another platform or storage location as needed.

CHAPTER 5
COLLABORATION WITH GOOGLE CHAT

- **Using Google Chat for Project Management**

Google Chat can be a valuable tool for project management, facilitating team communication, collaboration, and the organization of project-related information. Here are some ways to use Google Chat for project management:

1. **Create Dedicated Project Chats:**

- Start by creating dedicated chat rooms or group chats for each project. These chats serve as centralized hubs for project-related discussions, file sharing, and updates. Project members can easily access and contribute to these discussions.

2. **Set Clear Objectives:**

- Clearly define the objectives and scope of each project chat. Outline the project's goals, milestones, and deliverables, ensuring that everyone understands their roles and responsibilities.

3. **Use @Mentions:**

- Encourage the use of @mentions to grab the attention of specific team members. When you need someone's input or want to assign a task, simply type "@" followed by their name to notify them in the chat.

4. **File Sharing and Collaboration:**

- Share project-related documents, spreadsheets, and files directly within the chat. Google Drive integration allows for easy collaboration on files, with team members being able to edit and provide feedback in real time.

5. **Task Tracking:**

- You can use chat threads to create task lists, assign tasks to team members, and track progress. Utilize emojis or reactions to indicate task status (e.g., "In Progress" or "Completed").

6. **Calendar Integration:**

- Integrate Google Calendar to schedule project meetings, set deadlines, and send out meeting invites directly from your chat. This helps with time management and coordination.

7. **Notifications and Reminders:**

- Ensure that team members set up their notification preferences, such as receiving notifications for mentions and important updates. Use reminders to keep everyone on track with project deadlines.

8. **Custom Status Updates:**

- Encourage team members to use custom status updates to indicate their availability or provide brief project-related information. This can be a quick way to share progress or important updates with the team.

9. **Project Documentation:**

- Use chat threads to create and maintain project documentation. Share meeting minutes, project plans, and other essential documents directly in the chat for easy access.

10. **Archiving and Search:**

- Archive completed project chats to keep your chat list organized. When you need to reference past project discussions, use the search function to quickly locate specific conversations or details.

11. **Feedback and Discussions:**

- Promote open discussions and the sharing of ideas within the project chat. Encourage team members to ask questions, provide feedback, and share their insights.

12. **Integrate Additional Tools:**

- Depending on your project management needs, you can integrate other tools and apps with Google Chat. For instance, project management apps like Asana or Trello can be integrated to manage tasks and projects more comprehensively.

Using Google Chat for project management streamlines communication, keeps project-related information organized, and allows for real-time collaboration among team members. By creating a structured and efficient chat environment for each project, you can enhance productivity and project success.

- **Creating Shared Spaces and Rooms**

Shared spaces and rooms in Google Chat are collaborative areas where teams or groups can communicate, share information, and work together on projects or topics. Here's how to create shared spaces and rooms in Google Chat:

1. Access Google Chat:

- Start by logging in to your Google Chat account and accessing the main chat interface.

2. Create a Space (Room):

- **Creating a Space:** Google Chat uses the term "Space" for a shared area. To create a new Space:

- Click on the "+" icon in the left sidebar. This will open a menu with various options.

- Select "Create a space."

- Choose a name for the space. This name should reflect the topic or purpose of the shared area.
- Optionally, you can add a description to provide context for the space.
- Click "Create" to set up the space.

3. Add Members:

- After creating the space, you can add members to it. Click on the space you've just created, then click on the "Add People" button. You can add individuals or groups to the space. Members will be able to join the space and participate in discussions.

4. Customize the Space:

- You can customize the space by changing its image or color to make it easily recognizable. Click on the space, then click on the three vertical dots (more options) icon and choose "Space settings" to make these adjustments.

5. Create Rooms (Optional):

- **Creating Rooms within a Space:** Spaces can contain multiple rooms, which are subtopics or specific areas of focus within the broader space. To create a room within a space:
- Click on the space where you want to create a room.
- Click on the "+" icon within the space.

- Select "Create a room."
- Name the room and add a description if needed.
- Click "Create" to establish the room.

6. Customize Rooms:

- Just like spaces, you can customize rooms by changing their image, color, and description. Click on the room and access the room settings to make these adjustments.

7. Add Conversations and Content:

- Once your space and rooms are set up, you can begin conversations, share files, and collaborate on projects within them. Use chat threads to discuss specific topics or tasks.

8. Notifications and Activity:

- Keep an eye on the notifications and activity within your spaces and rooms to stay informed about new messages and updates.

9. Managing Access and Privacy:

- Be mindful of the access settings for your spaces and rooms. You can configure who can join, view, and participate in the discussions within these shared areas.

Creating shared spaces and rooms in Google Chat provides a structured and organized way for teams to collaborate, communicate, and work on projects or topics of interest. It streamlines communication, centralizes discussions, and enhances productivity by bringing relevant discussions into dedicated areas.

- **Collaborative Document Editing**

Google Chat seamlessly integrates with Google Workspace, allowing for collaborative document editing within the chat interface. Here's how you can use Google Chat for collaborative document editing:

1. Access Google Chat:

- Log in to your Google Chat account and access the main chat interface.

2. Start a Chat:

- Initiate a chat with the team members you want to collaborate with. You can create a one-on-one chat or a group chat, depending on the scope of your collaboration.

3. Share a Document:

- To begin collaborative document editing, share a Google Workspace document (e.g., Google Docs, Google Sheets, Google Slides) directly within the chat. You can do this by clicking on the attachment or paperclip icon in the chat conversation and selecting "Google Drive."

4. Select the Document:

- Choose the Google Workspace document you want to collaborate on from your Google Drive. You can also create a new document by selecting "Blank."

5. Collaborate in Real Time:

- Once the document is shared in the chat, you and your team members can open it and start editing collaboratively in real time. You can see each other's edits, comments, and suggestions as they happen.

6. Comment and Discuss:

- Use the comment feature within the document to discuss changes, provide feedback, and ask questions. Comment threads appear on the side of the document, allowing for threaded discussions.

7. Make Edits:

- Team members can make edits directly within the document, whether it's writing, adding data, or creating slides. The document automatically saves changes, and everyone with access can see the updates in real time.

8. Assign Tasks:

- You can assign specific tasks to team members by mentioning them in the chat conversation. For example, you can say, "John, could you review and edit section 3?" This way, responsibilities are clear and organized.

9. Notifications:

- Google Chat will send notifications to team members when comments or edits are made within the document. This ensures that everyone stays up to date on the progress.

10. Version History:

- Google Workspace documents keep a version history, allowing you to see changes made over time and revert to previous versions if necessary.

11. Chat Integration:

- You can continue discussions about the document in the chat while simultaneously editing the document. This integration streamlines communication and collaboration.

12. File Management:

- You can manage the document's access, sharing settings, and storage directly from the chat interface.

Collaborative document editing in Google Chat is a powerful feature for teams and organizations that need to work on shared documents in real time. It promotes seamless communication, efficient collaboration, and easy document management, making it an ideal solution for projects, reports, and any shared content that requires team input and coordination.

- **Integrating Chat with Google Workspace**

Google Chat is a central part of Google Workspace, providing powerful communication and collaboration features. Here's how to integrate Google Chat with Google Workspace for a seamless and productive experience:

1. Enable Google Chat:

- Google Chat is typically included in Google Workspace (formerly G Suite) by default. To use Google Chat, ensure that it's enabled for your organization. You can do this in the Google Admin Console under "Apps" and "Google Workspace" settings.

2. Access Google Chat:

- Log in to your Google Workspace account and access Google Chat. You can do this by visiting chat.google.com or clicking on the "Chat" icon in your Gmail account.

3. Use Chat in Gmail:

- Google Chat is integrated with Gmail, allowing you to access chat conversations from your Gmail interface. In Gmail, you'll find the Chat section on the left sidebar.

4. Access Chat on Mobile:

- Download the Google Chat mobile app from the Google Play Store (for Android) or the App Store (for iOS) to stay connected on the go.

5. Chat Features:

- Google Chat is closely integrated with other Google Workspace apps and services, such as Gmail, Google Drive, Google Calendar, and Google Meet. Utilize these integrations for seamless communication and collaboration.

6. Chat with Colleagues:

- Start chat conversations with colleagues by entering their email addresses or selecting them from your contact list.

7. Group Chats and Rooms:

- Create group chats or rooms to facilitate team discussions. These shared spaces are ideal for project coordination and topic-specific conversations.

8. File Sharing:

- Share files and documents from Google Drive directly in your chat conversations. Collaborate on documents in real time with integrated Google Workspace apps like Google Docs, Sheets, and Slides.

9. Video Meetings:

- Initiate video meetings using Google Meet directly from your chat conversations. You can schedule meetings, invite participants, and join meetings seamlessly.

10. Calendar Integration: - Google Chat integrates with Google Calendar, making it easy to schedule meetings and appointments right from the chat interface.

11. Collaboration and Editing: - Collaboratively edit documents in real time within chat conversations. Multiple users can work on the same document simultaneously.

12. Access Control and Permissions: - Manage access and permissions for chat conversations and shared documents, ensuring that the right people have the appropriate level of access.

13. Notifications and Alerts: - Configure notification settings to receive alerts for important messages, mentions, and updates.

14. Archive and Search: - Archive chat conversations for future reference and use the search function to quickly locate past discussions.

15. Admin Controls: - Google Workspace administrators can configure and manage settings for Google Chat at the organizational level, ensuring security and compliance.

Integrating Google Chat with Google Workspace offers a unified communication and collaboration platform for organizations. It streamlines workflows, enhances productivity, and makes it easy for teams to connect, share information, and collaborate effectively.

- **Effective Team Collaboration Tips**

Collaboration is essential for productive team communication, and Google Chat provides a platform for effective collaboration. Here are some tips for promoting successful team collaboration in Google Chat:

1. Create Dedicated Spaces:

- Organize your team discussions by creating dedicated spaces or rooms for each project, department, or topic. This helps keep conversations focused and makes it easy to find specific discussions.

2. Set Clear Objectives:

- Clearly define the objectives and goals of each chat room or conversation. Ensure that team members understand the purpose and scope of their collaboration.

3. Use @Mentions:

- Use @mentions to get the attention of specific team members. It's an effective way to assign tasks, request feedback, or direct questions to the right individuals.

4. Share Documents and Files:

- Share project-related documents and files directly within the chat. Google Drive integration allows for seamless collaboration on documents in real time.

5. Task Tracking:

- Create task lists within chat conversations to keep track of action items, deadlines, and responsibilities. Use emojis or reactions to indicate task status.

6. Calendar Integration:

- Integrate Google Chat with Google Calendar to schedule meetings, set reminders, and keep track of important dates and appointments.

7. Notifications and Alerts:

- Configure notification settings to receive timely alerts for important messages and updates. Ensure that team members understand how to manage their notification preferences.

8. Communication Etiquette:

- Encourage clear and concise communication within chat conversations. Use descriptive chat titles and message subjects to help keep discussions organized.

9. Status Updates:

- Utilize custom status updates to indicate your availability or provide context to your team. For example, you can set your status to "In a Meeting" or "Out of Office."

10. Archiving and Search: - Archive completed chat conversations to keep your chat list tidy. Use the search function to quickly locate past conversations or specific details when needed.

11. Collaborative Document Editing: - Take advantage of Google Chat's integration with Google Workspace to collaboratively edit documents within the chat. It streamlines real-time collaboration on projects and reports.

12. Polls and Surveys: - Use chat to conduct polls or surveys to gather input and feedback from team members. Google Forms can be integrated for this purpose.

13. Encourage Feedback: - Foster an environment where team members feel comfortable providing feedback and sharing ideas. Constructive criticism can lead to improvements and innovation.

14. Integration with Other Tools: - Integrate other productivity and project management tools as needed. Google Chat offers third-party integrations for additional features and functionalities.

15. Document Best Practices: - Establish best practices for document and file management within the chat. Encourage version control, clear naming conventions, and proper categorization.

16. Regular Check-Ins: - Schedule regular team check-ins and update meetings using Google Chat. This helps keep everyone aligned and informed.

17. Training and Support: - Provide training and support to team members to ensure they are proficient in using Google Chat's features effectively.

By following these tips and best practices, you can leverage Google Chat to foster a collaborative and productive team environment. Effective collaboration results in improved communication, increased productivity, and better project outcomes.

CHAPTER 6

SECURITY AND PRIVACY IN GOOGLE CHAT

- **Understanding Chat Security Features**

Security is paramount in communication and collaboration tools, and Google Chat offers several security features to protect your conversations and data. Here's an overview of some key security features in Google Chat:

1. **End-to-End Encryption (E2EE):** Google Chat offers end-to-end encryption for one-on-one conversations, meaning that only you and the recipient can read the messages. This ensures the privacy and security of your sensitive information.

2. **Data Encryption:** Chat data is encrypted in transit, making it difficult for unauthorized parties to intercept or access your messages as they travel between devices and Google's servers.

3. **Authentication:** Google Chat uses secure authentication methods to ensure that only authorized users can access and participate in chats. This helps prevent unauthorized access to your conversations.

4. **Access Controls:** Google Chat provides administrators with tools to control user access, enforce security policies, and manage

permissions within the organization. Admins can set user roles and control data access.

5. **Compliance and Auditing:** Google Chat is designed to meet various compliance standards, making it suitable for organizations with specific regulatory requirements. Admins can access audit logs and reports for compliance purposes.

6. **Two-Factor Authentication (2FA):** You can enable two-factor authentication for your Google Chat account, adding an extra layer of security. With 2FA, users must provide a second verification step (such as a one-time code) in addition to their password.

7. **Phishing Protection:** Google Chat includes built-in phishing protection to detect and block suspicious links and attachments. This helps prevent users from falling victim to phishing attacks.

8. **Data Retention Policies:** Admins can set data retention policies to control how long chat data is stored. This can help organizations meet legal and regulatory requirements while ensuring that chat data isn't retained longer than necessary.

9. **Mobile Device Management (MDM):** Google Workspace provides mobile device management capabilities, allowing administrators to secure and manage mobile devices used for

Google Chat. They can enforce policies like passcode requirements and remote wipe.

10. **Third-Party Integrations:** If you use third-party apps and integrations within Google Chat, it's essential to understand their security features and data handling practices. Only integrate trusted applications.

11. **Screen Sharing Controls:** When using Google Meet for video conferencing within Google Chat, you can control screen sharing and participant access to enhance meeting security.

12. **Privacy Settings:** Users can customize their privacy settings to control who can add them to groups and communicate with them. This adds a layer of control over who can interact with you in Google Chat.

13. **Secure APIs:** Google Chat's APIs and integration framework are designed with security in mind, enabling developers to create safe and secure integrations.

14. **User Education:** Ensure that users are educated on security best practices, such as recognizing phishing attempts, using strong passwords, and reporting suspicious activity.

It's essential to work closely with your organization's IT and security teams to implement and configure these security features in Google Chat to meet your specific security and compliance requirements. By doing so, you can use Google Chat with confidence, knowing that your communications are secure and protected.

- **Two-Factor Authentication for Chat**

Two-Factor Authentication (2FA) is an additional layer of security that helps protect your Google Chat account from unauthorized access. Enabling 2FA ensures that even if someone has your password, they won't be able to access your account without the second verification step. Here's how to set up 2FA for Google Chat:

1. Access Your Google Account:

- Start by logging in to your Google Account. You can do this by visiting https://myaccount.google.com and signing in with your credentials.

2. Go to Security Settings:

- In your Google Account, navigate to the "Security" tab on the left-hand menu.

3. Enable 2-Step Verification:

- Under the "Signing in to Google" section, you'll find the "2-Step Verification" option. Click on it.

4. Start the 2FA Setup:

- Click the "Get started" button to begin the setup process.

5. Verify Your Identity:

- Google will ask you to sign in again for security purposes. Enter your password and proceed.

6. Add a Second Step:

- You'll be prompted to add a second step for verification. You can choose from several options, including receiving a text message or using the Google Authenticator app.

7. Set Up a Backup Option:

- Google recommends setting up a backup option in case you can't access your primary 2FA method. You can add a backup phone number or generate backup codes that you can use if needed.

8. Complete the Setup:

- Follow the on-screen instructions to complete the setup of 2FA. You'll typically receive a verification code on your selected device or app to confirm your identity.

9. Confirm 2FA:

- Once 2FA is set up, you'll receive a confirmation that it's active. You can now use 2FA when logging in to your Google Chat account.

10. Logging in with 2FA: - When logging in to Google Chat or other Google services, you'll be prompted to enter the second verification step, which may involve receiving a code on your mobile device or using an authentication app. This added layer of security ensures that only authorized users can access your account.

11. Recovery Codes: - Make sure to generate and securely store recovery codes that you can use if you ever lose access to your primary 2FA method. These codes are a critical backup for account recovery.

Enabling 2FA for Google Chat is a vital step in enhancing the security of your account. It significantly reduces the risk of unauthorized access and protects your sensitive information. Be sure to store your backup codes and securely manage your 2FA settings to ensure continued access to your account.

- **End-to-End Encryption and Privacy**

End-to-End Encryption (E2EE) is a security feature that ensures that only the sender and the recipient of a message can read its contents. In the context of Google Chat, here's what you need to know about E2EE and privacy:

1. E2EE in Google Chat:

- Google Chat offers end-to-end encryption for one-on-one conversations. This means that the messages you exchange with another user are encrypted on your device, transmitted in encrypted form, and only decrypted on the recipient's device. Google does not have access to the unencrypted content of these messages.

2. Limitations of E2EE:

- While E2EE provides strong privacy and security for one-on-one conversations, it's important to note that group chats and rooms in Google Chat do not currently support end-to-end encryption. Messages in group chats and rooms are encrypted in transit and at rest, but they can be accessed by Google administrators for purposes such as compliance and data management.

3. User Authentication:

- Google Chat uses secure user authentication methods to ensure that only authorized users can access and participate in chats. This adds an important layer of security to prevent unauthorized access.

4. Secure Data Transmission:

- Chat data is encrypted in transit, which means that messages are protected as they travel between devices and Google's servers. This encryption helps prevent eavesdropping or interception of messages.

5. Security Best Practices:

- To enhance privacy and security in Google Chat, it's important to follow security best practices. This includes setting strong and unique passwords, enabling two-factor authentication

(2FA), and being cautious about sharing sensitive information in chats.

6. Privacy Controls:

- Google Chat provides privacy controls that allow you to customize who can add you to groups, start conversations with you, or see your online status. These controls help you manage your privacy within the platform.

7. Legal and Compliance Requirements:

- Google Chat is designed to meet various legal and compliance standards, making it suitable for organizations with specific regulatory requirements. Administrators can access audit logs and reports for compliance purposes.

8. User Education:

- It's essential to educate users about privacy and security best practices when using Google Chat. Users should be aware of the limitations of E2EE in group chats and rooms and take precautions when discussing sensitive information in these contexts.

9. Third-Party Integrations:

- If you use third-party applications or integrations within Google Chat, it's crucial to review their privacy policies and security practices to ensure your data is handled securely.

In summary, Google Chat's use of end-to-end encryption for one-on-one conversations enhances privacy and security by ensuring that your messages are only accessible to you and the recipient. However, it's important to be aware of the limitations in group chats and rooms, and to follow best practices to protect your privacy and sensitive information. Users and administrators should work together to create a secure and privacy-aware environment within Google Chat.

- **Reporting and Blocking Suspicious Activity**

To maintain a secure and safe chat environment, it's essential to know how to report and block suspicious activity in Google Chat. If you encounter behavior or content that raises concerns, here's what you can do:

1. Reporting Suspicious Activity:

- **Unwanted or Inappropriate Messages:** If you receive unwanted, spammy, or inappropriate messages in Google Chat, you can report the conversation for review.

- **Phishing or Suspicious Links:** If someone sends you links that appear to be phishing attempts or potentially harmful, report the message to alert Google.

- **Harassment or Abusive Behavior:** If you're the target of harassment or abusive behavior in a chat, report the individual or conversation to address the issue.

- **Reporting Security Concerns:** If you suspect a security concern or unauthorized access to your account, report it immediately.

2. How to Report Suspicious Activity:

- In Google Chat, open the conversation that contains the suspicious activity.
- Click on the three vertical dots (more options) icon within the chat conversation.
- Select "Report" from the dropdown menu.
- Follow the on-screen prompts to provide details about the suspicious activity.
- Google will review your report and take appropriate action based on its policies and guidelines.

3. Blocking Users:

- If you want to prevent further communication with a specific user who is engaging in suspicious or unwelcome behavior, you can block them.
- Open the chat conversation with the user you want to block.
- Click on the three vertical dots (more options) icon within the chat conversation.
- Select "Block" from the dropdown menu.

- Once blocked, the user won't be able to contact you through Google Chat.

4. Contact Support:

- In more severe cases, or if you believe there's a serious security threat, you can contact Google Support for assistance. Google can provide guidance and support in dealing with such issues.

5. Privacy Settings:

- You can manage your privacy settings to control who can add you to groups, start conversations with you, or see your online status. Adjust these settings to enhance your privacy and security.

6. User Education:

- It's crucial to educate users about recognizing and reporting suspicious activity. Ensure that team members are aware of the reporting and blocking features in Google Chat.

By reporting and blocking suspicious activity in Google Chat, you contribute to maintaining a safe and secure chat environment. Google takes such reports seriously and acts promptly to address inappropriate or harmful behavior within the platform.

- **Best Practices for Keeping Your Chats Secure**

Ensuring the security of your chats in Google Chat is essential to protect sensitive information and maintain a safe online environment. Here are best practices for keeping your chats secure:

1. Use Strong, Unique Passwords:

- Use complex passwords that are difficult for others to guess. Combine uppercase and lowercase letters, numbers, and special characters. Avoid using easily guessable information like birthdays or common words.

2. Enable Two-Factor Authentication (2FA):

- Enable 2FA for your Google account. This adds an extra layer of security, requiring you to provide a second verification step, such as a one-time code, in addition to your password.

3. Be Cautious with Links and Attachments:

- Avoid clicking on links or opening attachments from unknown or suspicious sources. Phishing attempts often involve deceptive links that can compromise your security.

4. Verify Contact Identities:

- Before sharing sensitive information, verify the identity of the person you are communicating with. Confirm that they are who they claim to be, especially in business or professional contexts.

5. Encrypt Sensitive Information:

- When sharing sensitive information, consider encrypting it before sending. Encryption tools and services can add an extra layer of protection to your data.

6. Use End-to-End Encryption:

- For highly sensitive one-on-one conversations, use the end-to-end encryption (E2EE) feature in Google Chat to ensure that only you and the recipient can read the messages.

7. Keep Software Updated:

- Ensure that you are using the latest version of Google Chat and that your operating system and software are up to date with security patches and updates.

8. Avoid Public Wi-Fi for Sensitive Chats:

- Avoid using public Wi-Fi networks for chats that involve sensitive or confidential information. These networks can be less secure, making it easier for others to intercept your communications.

9. Secure Your Device:

- Secure your computer or mobile device with a password or PIN to prevent unauthorized access to your chat history.

10. Use Encrypted Messaging Apps for Extra Security: - Consider using encrypted messaging apps for particularly sensitive discussions. Apps like Signal or WhatsApp provide strong encryption and security features.

11. Monitor for Suspicious Activity: - Keep an eye out for any unusual or suspicious activity in your chats, such as unexpected file transfers or unknown participants in group chats.

12. Set Privacy Controls: - Customize your privacy settings to control who can add you to groups, start conversations with you, or see your online status. Adjust these settings according to your comfort level.

13. Educate Team Members: - In a business or team environment, educate your colleagues or team members about security best practices in chat. Awareness and vigilance can go a long way in preventing security breaches.

14. Report and Block Suspicious Activity: - Familiarize yourself with the process of reporting and blocking suspicious activity. Use these features when necessary to protect your security and privacy.

By following these best practices, you can significantly enhance the security of your chats in Google Chat, whether for personal, professional, or team communication. Maintaining a proactive and security-conscious approach is crucial to protect your information and maintain a safe online environment.

- **Advanced Tips and Tricks and FAQs**

1. **Keyboard Shortcuts:** Learn keyboard shortcuts to navigate Google Chat more efficiently. For example, press "Ctrl + /" on Windows or "Cmd + /" on Mac to access a list of available shortcuts.

2. **Integrate Bots and Automation:** Explore chatbots and automation tools to streamline tasks and processes. Bots can perform actions like scheduling, file sharing, and data retrieval.

3. **Slash Commands:** Utilize slash commands to quickly perform actions in chat. For example, "/meet" can start a Google Meet video call, or "/drive" can help you search for files in Google Drive.

4. **Mentions and Notifications:** Master the art of mentions and notifications to ensure important messages get the attention they deserve. Use "@mentions" to grab someone's attention, and set notification preferences for key conversations.

5. **Advanced Search:** Learn advanced search techniques to find specific chat messages and conversations more efficiently. You can use search operators to filter results.

6. **Starred Messages:** Use the "Star" feature to mark important messages or conversations. You can easily find starred messages in your chat list for quick reference.

7. **Reactions and Emojis:** Make use of reactions and emojis to add nuance to your messages and express emotions. You can react to messages with emojis to provide quick feedback.

8. **Editing and Deleting Messages:** Familiarize yourself with how to edit or delete messages in chat. Edit messages for corrections or clarification, and delete messages when needed.

FAQs (Frequently Asked Questions) about Google Chat

1. Is Google Chat the same as Google Hangouts?

- No, Google Chat and Google Hangouts are separate apps, although they share some features. Google Chat is part of Google Workspace and focuses on professional and team communication, while Google Hangouts is a consumer-oriented messaging app.

2. Can I use Google Chat for personal communication?

- Yes, you can use Google Chat for personal communication. You can send messages to individuals or create group chats for friends and family.

3. Can I use Google Chat offline?

- Google Chat primarily requires an internet connection, but you can access recent conversations in "Offline mode" in the Google Chat mobile app or via Google Chat in Gmail.

4. How do I set up a group chat or room in Google Chat?

- To create a group chat or room, open Google Chat, click on the "+" button, and select "Create a room." Name your room, add members, and customize settings.

5. Is Google Chat available on mobile devices?

- Yes, Google Chat has mobile apps for both Android and iOS, allowing you to stay connected on your smartphones and tablets.

6. Can I make voice or video calls in Google Chat?

- Yes, Google Chat integrates with Google Meet, so you can make voice and video calls directly from your chat conversations.

7. What's the difference between Google Chat and Google Meet?

- Google Chat is primarily for text-based chat and file sharing, while Google Meet is focused on video conferencing and virtual meetings. However, they are integrated, so you can start video calls from Google Chat.

8. Is Google Chat secure for business communication?

- Google Chat provides security features like end-to-end encryption for one-on-one chats and robust authentication. For additional security, organizations can configure settings and access controls in Google Workspace.

9. How do I integrate third-party apps with Google Chat?

- You can explore Google Chat's third-party integrations by visiting the "Chat App Marketplace" in the Google Chat web app. Choose from a variety of apps to enhance functionality and productivity.

10. How can I export chat history from Google Chat? - Google Chat allows you to export your chat history. In the chat conversation, click on the three vertical dots (more options), select "Export chat," and follow the instructions to save your chat history.

CHAPTER 7

INTEGRATING GOOGLE CHAT INTO YOUR WORKFLOWS

- **Using Chat for Remote Work and Virtual Meetings**

Google Chat is a versatile tool for remote work and virtual meetings, enabling effective communication and collaboration in a distributed work environment. Here's how to make the most of Google Chat for remote work and virtual meetings:

1. Chat for Quick Messaging:

- Use Google Chat for quick one-on-one or group messaging to communicate with colleagues and teammates. It's an efficient way to exchange information and updates throughout the day.

2. Create Chat Rooms:

- Set up chat rooms or shared spaces for specific projects, teams, or topics. Rooms facilitate ongoing discussions and collaboration in a dedicated workspace.

3. Schedule Virtual Meetings:

- Seamlessly integrate Google Meet with Google Chat to schedule and join virtual meetings. You can start a video call from a chat conversation with a single click.

4. Share Files and Documents:

- Share documents, spreadsheets, and presentations from Google Drive directly within chat conversations. Collaboratively edit files in real time, enhancing productivity.

5. Task Management:

- Use chat to create and manage task lists. Assign tasks to team members, set deadlines, and track progress within the chat interface.

6. Mobile Accessibility:

- Download the Google Chat mobile app to stay connected and communicate on the go. It's a convenient way to participate in work-related discussions from your mobile device.

7. Integrations with Other Apps:

- Explore third-party app integrations available in Google Chat to extend its functionality. Integrate project management tools, CRM systems, or other apps that streamline your remote work processes.

8. Notifications and Reminders:

- Customize notification settings to receive timely alerts for important messages, mentions, or upcoming virtual meetings. Ensure you don't miss critical updates.

9. Archive and Search:

- Archive chat conversations when they are no longer active but need to be retained for reference. The search feature helps you quickly find past discussions and information.

10. Privacy and Security: - Configure your privacy settings to control who can start conversations with you and see your online status. Familiarize yourself with security best practices to protect sensitive information.

11. Screen Sharing and Collaboration: - During virtual meetings, utilize screen sharing and collaborative document editing to enhance team collaboration and ensure everyone is on the same page.

12. Regular Check-Ins: - Schedule regular virtual check-ins and update meetings with your team. Google Chat's integration with Google Calendar simplifies this process.

13. Efficient Remote Onboarding: - Use chat for remote onboarding of new team members. Create an onboarding room, share resources, and guide newcomers through the company's processes and tools.

14. Conduct Polls and Surveys: - Use chat to conduct polls or surveys to gather input and feedback from team members. Google Forms can be integrated for this purpose.

15. Monitor Progress: - Keep an eye on team progress by following discussions in chat rooms and tracking task lists. Provide feedback and guidance as necessary.

By leveraging the features and integrations within Google Chat, you can enhance remote work and virtual meetings, ensuring that teams collaborate effectively, stay organized, and maintain productivity, no matter where they are located.

- **Chat and Project Management Tools Integration**

Integrating Google Chat with project management tools streamlines communication, collaboration, and task tracking. Here's how to integrate Google Chat with project management tools effectively:

1. **Select the Right Project Management Tool:**

- Choose a project management tool that offers integration with Google Chat. Popular options include Asana, Trello, and Monday.com.

2. **Install the Integration:**

- Access the integration marketplace within your project management tool. Look for the Google Chat integration and install it.

3. **Authorize Access:**

- Follow the prompts to authorize the integration to access your Google Chat account. This ensures that the project management tool can send updates and notifications to chat.

4. **Create Projects and Tasks:**

- Create projects and tasks within your project management tool as usual. Assign tasks to team members and set deadlines.

5. **Link to Chat Rooms:**

- In your project management tool, link relevant projects or tasks to specific Google Chat rooms or chat conversations. This connection enables real-time updates.

6. **Receive Notifications:**

- As progress is made or changes occur in your projects, your linked chat rooms will receive notifications. Team members will stay informed without leaving Google Chat.

7. **Discuss Projects in Chat:**

- Use Google Chat rooms for project-related discussions, questions, and updates. The chat room serves as a central hub for communication.

Chat and Calendar Integration

Integrating Google Chat with Google Calendar streamlines scheduling and enhances event planning. Here's how to make the most of this integration:

1. **Access Google Chat in Gmail:**

- Open Google Chat within Gmail, and access the "Chat" section on the left sidebar.

2. **Connect to Google Calendar:**

- Ensure that your Google Calendar is connected to your Google Chat account. This is typically done by default if you're using Google Workspace.

3. **Schedule Meetings:**

- In Google Chat, start a conversation with the person or group you want to meet with. Click on the "+ icon" in the chat text box and select "Schedule a meeting."

4. **Add Event Details:**

- A calendar event will be created with the chat participants and title pre-filled. You can customize the date, time, location, and other details.

5. **Set Reminders:**

- Configure reminders for your meeting, such as a notification before the event. Participants will receive reminders in chat and through Google Calendar.

6. **Join the Meeting:**

- When the meeting time arrives, click on the "Join" button in the chat conversation to start the Google Meet video call.

7. **Automatic Event Updates:**

- Any changes made to the meeting in Google Calendar, such as rescheduling or canceling, will be reflected in the chat conversation.

8. **Access Calendar Events:**

- View and manage upcoming calendar events from Google Chat by clicking the "Calendar" icon in the chat sidebar. This provides quick access to your schedule.

9. **Meeting Agendas:**

- Use the chat conversation to share meeting agendas, documents, and important information in advance of the meeting.

Integrating Google Chat with project management tools and Google Calendar enhances productivity and organization by centralizing communication and scheduling. Team members can seamlessly collaborate on projects and schedule meetings without switching between multiple apps.

- **Third-Party App Integrations**

Google Chat offers a wide range of third-party app integrations to enhance its functionality and support various business needs. Here's how to effectively integrate third-party apps into Google Chat:

1. **Explore the Chat App Marketplace:**

- Access the Chat App Marketplace within Google Chat or Google Workspace. It provides a catalog of available third-party apps and integrations.

2. **Choose the Right Apps:**

- Browse the marketplace to discover apps that align with your specific requirements. Popular categories include project management, document collaboration, and customer relationship management (CRM).

3. **Install and Authorize Integrations:**

- Select the app you want to integrate and follow the installation prompts. You'll typically need to authorize the integration to access your Google Chat account.

4. **Customize Settings:**

- Adjust the integration settings to fit your needs. This might involve specifying which chat rooms or conversations the app should interact with.

5. **Use Integration Features:**

- Once the integration is active, utilize its features within Google Chat. For example, you might use a CRM integration to access customer data or a project management tool to update tasks.

6. **Collaborate Seamlessly:**

- Collaborate with team members using the integrated apps to streamline workflows and centralize communication.

7. **Stay Informed:**

- Keep up to date with the latest developments in third-party app integrations to discover new tools that can further enhance your Google Chat experience.

Future Developments and Trends in Google Chat

Google Chat is continuously evolving to meet the changing needs of users and organizations. Here are some future developments and trends you can expect to see in Google Chat:

1. **Enhanced Automation:** Google Chat will likely offer more automation features, including chatbots and AI-driven assistants that can perform routine tasks and answer queries.

2. **Deeper Integrations:** Google will continue to expand its integration ecosystem, allowing for seamless connections with more third-party apps and services.

3. **Improved Mobile Experience:** Expect enhancements in the mobile app, making it even more convenient and feature-rich for users on the go.

4. **Advanced Security Features:** Google Chat will likely introduce additional security features and compliance tools to cater to the needs of organizations with strict data protection requirements.

5. **Integration with Google Workspace:** Integration with other Google Workspace tools, such as Google Drive and Google

Docs, will become even more seamless to enhance collaboration and productivity.

6. **AI-Driven Chat Features:** Anticipate AI-driven features for smart suggestions, automated message categorization, and improved search capabilities.

7. **Expansion of E2EE:** Google may expand end-to-end encryption to cover group chats and rooms, further enhancing privacy and security.

8. **New Collaboration Tools:** Google Chat may introduce new collaboration tools to support emerging trends in remote work and virtual collaboration.

9. **Enhanced Notifications:** More flexible and customizable notification settings to help users stay informed without overwhelming them with alerts.

10. **Voice and Video Improvements:** Expect improvements in voice and video calls, including higher quality, additional features, and better integration with Google Meet.

As Google Chat continues to evolve, users can look forward to a more feature-rich and integrated platform that caters to the evolving needs of remote work, collaboration, and communication in a digital-first world. Stay updated on Google Workspace announcements to make the most of these future developments.

CONCLUSION

In conclusion, Google Chat is a powerful communication and collaboration platform that offers a wide array of features and capabilities for both personal and professional use. From understanding the basics of Google Chat to leveraging advanced tips and tricks, this comprehensive guide equips you with the knowledge to master the platform. Here are the key takeaways:

- **Getting Started**: You've learned how to set up your Google Chat account, navigate the interface, and customize your profile.

- **Communication**: You know how to add contacts, send messages, and utilize features like status and presence, emojis, and reactions.

- **Features**: You're familiar with text chat, group messaging, voice and video calls, file sharing, and integrating Google Chat with other Google apps.

- **Settings and Organization**: You've gained insights into managing notifications, organizing chats and conversations, pinning important chats, and archiving and searching chats.

- **Security and Privacy**: You understand the importance of end-to-end encryption, two-factor authentication, and other security measures to protect your chats.

- **Professional Use**: You're equipped to use Google Chat for project management, creating shared spaces and rooms, collaborative document editing, and integration with Google Workspace.
- **Effective Communication**: You know how to ensure secure and efficient communication, and you're aware of the methods to report and block suspicious activity.
- **Advanced Tips and Tricks**: You've learned advanced techniques, keyboard shortcuts, integrations with third-party apps, and how to make the most of Google Chat for remote work and virtual meetings.
- **Integration**: You know how to integrate Google Chat with project management tools and Google Calendar to streamline your workflows.
- **Future Developments and Trends**: You're aware of the future trends and developments to expect in Google Chat, including enhanced automation, improved mobile experiences, and advanced security features.

Google Chat is a dynamic and evolving platform that can significantly enhance your communication and collaboration capabilities. By following best practices and staying informed about future developments, you'll be well-prepared to harness the full potential of Google Chat for your personal and professional needs.

www.ingramcontent.com/pod-product-compliance
Lightning Source LLC
LaVergne TN
LVHW022009200926
848481LV00007B/2311